The KidChat Series

KidChat
222 Creative Questions to Spark Conversations

KidChat Too!
212 All-New Questions to Ignite the Imagination

KidChat Gone Wild!
202 Creative Questions to Unleash the Imagination

KidChat Oh, the Places to Go!
204 Creative Questions to Let the Imagination Travel

The Question Guys™

212 All-New Questions to Ignite the Imagination

Bret Nicholaus and Paul Lowrie

A Deborah Brodie Book ROARING BROOK PRESS * New York

For Grant, from Dad

Text copyright © 2004, 2007 Bret Nicholaus and Paul Lowrie

A Deborah Brodie Book
Published by Roaring Brook Press
Roaring Brook Press is a division of Holtzbrinck Publishing Holdings Limited Partnership
175 Fifth Avenue, New York, NY 10010

Distributed in Canada by H. B. Fenn and Company, Ltd.

Library of Congress Cataloging-in-Publication Data

Nicholaus, Bret.
KidChat too! : all-new questions to fuel young minds and mouths / Bret Nicholaus and Paul Lowrie. — 1st ed.
  p. cm.
"A Deborah Brodie book."
Originally published: Yankton, S.D. : Questmarc, 2004.
ISBN-13: 978-1-59643-315-1
ISBN-10: 1-59643-315-9
1. Children's questions and answers. 2. Curiosities and wonders—Juvenile literature.
3. Handbooks, vade-mecums, etc.—Juvenile literature. 4. Creative thinking in children.
I. Lowrie, Paul. II. Title.
AG195.N535 2007
031.02—dc22
2006039721

10 9 8 7 6 5 4 3 2 1

Roaring Brook Press books are available for special promotions and premiums.
For details, contact: Director of Special Markets, Holtzbrinck Publishers.

Book design by Míkael Vilhjálmsson
Printed in the United States of America
First Roaring Brook Press edition October 2007

welcome again!

You asked for it, so you got it! Over the last several years, as *KidChat* has made its way into homes, cars, and schools around the country, we have received nearly constant requests for a sequel to that book. As we were thrilled that *KidChat* made the big splash that it did, we were equally thrilled to have the opportunity to write yet another book of fun, creative, and thought-provoking questions for kids (and, for that matter, kids-at-heart of all ages). *KidChat Too!* is the final result of our work over the last few months.

While the questions in this book are completely different from those in the first book, the overall style remains nearly the same—making it the perfect companion book to the original. By the same token, for those who never saw or used the first *KidChat* book, *KidChat Too!* can be enjoyed just as much completely on its own. This book of all-new questions will give kids, parents, and teachers plenty of food for thought—and, yes, plenty of food for talk!

Kids will love using *KidChat Too!* with their friends, as it facilitates fun discussions about things they probably don't think about every day, and, in fact, may never have thought about in the past. It can be used at school with their peers or in the home with their parents. It works equally well at the dinner table and on long trips in the car. It's a favorite for sleepovers, parties, and children's groups, and is an ideal tool for creative writing. And as with the first book, teachers will find this book to be an invaluable source for a "Question of the Day"—a popular way to get the morning started in classrooms around the country.

There is no particular order to the questions, so kids can open to any page at any time and read whatever question they see there. We would also like to point out that there are no wrong answers to these questions—only opinions. Oftentimes, kids will discover that the way they think changes from day to day; the answer given for a question today may be completely different from their answer to the same question tomorrow. Whether their answer remains the same or changes, it doesn't matter a bit—the simple goal of this book is to get kids thinking and talking in a way that makes it incredibly entertaining and educational for everyone involved. In the process of asking and answering the questions contained in this collection, kids and adults will learn an amazing amount about themselves, others, and the incredible world in which we all live.

Regardless of where or how you use these questions, we believe you will find *KidChat Too!* to be a truly unique book of kid-friendly material that kids (and adults!) will want to use over and over again. So why wait another minute for the fun to begin? Turn the page and start asking some questions.

Bret Nicholaus and Paul Lowrie, The Question Guys™

special note

Every few pages, kids will notice a heading that says "imagination igniter." These words indicate that the question below it is specially designed to stimulate very creative thinking and the full-blown use of their imaginations.

Approximately every twenty questions, kids will see another heading that says "THINK ABOUT IT . . ."; the page contains a quotation from which we believe kids can learn something very important about life. You'll notice that each of these pages features the question, "What do these words mean for your life?" To get the full benefit of the quotation and its implications for each and every child, we encourage parents or teachers to have fun discussing the quote with their kid/student.

"Every child is born blessed with a vivid imagination.
But just as a muscle grows weak with disuse,
so the bright imagination of a child will fade in
later years if he ceases to exercise it."

❋⟨ WALT DISNEY ⟩❋

1

IF YOU WERE ASKED for the summer to help a national park ranger do his or her job, what would you hope to see or do more than anything else during your summer in the park?

2

SUPPOSE THAT once a week, on Saturday mornings, a mail delivery truck would pull up to your house and you'd be handed a package with something inside just for you. Assuming that each week the package had to have the same type of thing inside, what would you want your weekly package to contain? (Example: a different videotape each week.)

IMAGINATION IGNITER

3

If you had to paint a message on the roof of your house that could be seen by anyone driving or walking by, what message would you paint there?

→ **4** ←

IF YOU HAD TO create a brand-new letter to be added to the current alphabet, what would this new letter look like and how would you pronounce it?

→ **5** ←

SUPPOSE THAT for one week, instead of saying "hi" to someone you had to greet them with the sound of a farm animal. What farm animal's sound would you choose for your greeting?

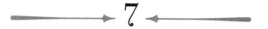

6

WHAT IS something you really like that most other kids your age don't like?

7

THINK FOR A FEW moments of all the different forms of transportation (planes, trains, cars, boats, bikes, taxicabs, buses, motorcycles, etc.). If you had to describe your personality in terms of a type of transportation, which type would best describe you?

ImaGINaTION
IGNITER

→ 8 ←

If you had to write your own personal definition of the word success, what would it be?

9

IF YOU WERE a teacher, what is one book that you would tell your whole class to read? Why do you think this would be an important book for students to read and then discuss as a class?

10

IN YOUR OPINION, what is the nicest thing you've ever done for someone else? Why did you do it? How did the other person respond or act when you did it?

11

FOR EACH OF THE four seasons (spring, summer, fall, winter), what is your favorite sound?

12

IF YOU COULD TAKE a ride on the back of any animal, what animal would you choose?

13

IF YOU WERE A cartographer (someone whose job it is to make maps or charts) and could make a map or chart of anything you wanted, what would you want your map or chart to feature? (Examples: a map showing the location of the 25 biggest amusement parks in the country, or a chart that shows the speeds of the 25 fastest roller coasters in the world.)

— 14 —

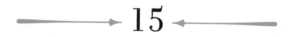

IF YOU COULD SIT down and talk for one hour with any past president of the United States, which president would you choose? What are three specific questions you would want him to answer for you?

— 15 —

IF YOU HAD TO DO a job someday that required you to wear a uniform, what job would you want more than any other? (You may choose any job except for that of a professional athlete.)

— → 16 ← —

WHAT DO YOU think will be the most difficult part of being an adult someday?

— → 17 ← —

SUPPOSE THAT instead of having a name, you had a letter, and people throughout your life would always refer to you as that letter. What letter of the alphabet would you want to take the place of your name?

THINK ABOUT IT . . .

→ 18 ←

"The best things in life aren't things."
—*Ann Landers, newspaper columnist/writer*

What do these words mean for your life?
Talk about it with your parents or a teacher.

— → 19 ← —

IF YOU WERE IN charge of picking the next host country for an Olympic Games (that is, the country where the games will be held), which country would you choose?

— → 20 ← —

WHAT IS THE hardest thing you've ever had to memorize? How did you do it?

21

IF YOU COULD BE the mayor of any city in the country, what city would you choose and what would be your first goal for that city? How might you go about trying to achieve this goal?

22

IF YOU HAD TO choose one of the following three items which you could use to make anything creative you wanted, which one would you pick: a box of 100 soda straws, a 75-foot roll of aluminum foil, or a bag of 50 rubber bands?

23

WHAT IF AN APPLE tasted like a banana? Or what if a banana tasted like an apple? If you could choose any fruit at all and make it taste like another fruit, what fruit would you choose and what fruit would it now taste like?

24

IF YOU COULD experience a sailing adventure on any river, lake, or ocean in the world, what body of water would you choose for your adventure?

25

IF YOU WERE given $500 that you in turn had to use to help somebody else, for whom and for what purpose would you want the money to be used?

26

TAKE A FEW seconds and look at a map of the United States. Which state, in your opinion, has the coolest-looking shape? If you could create anything at all in the shape of this state, what would you make? (Example: a swimming pool in the shape of Florida.)

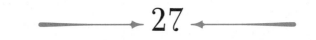

27

IF a professional carpenter offered to build from wood anything you wanted—anything at all—what would you want to have built for you?

28

IF YOU WERE a professional athlete, would you rather be extremely fast or extremely strong?

29

IF THE DOOR TO your bedroom could be in any shape you wanted other than the standard rectangle, what shape would you choose for your door?

IMAGINATION IGNITER

→ 30 ←

If you were a train engineer and had to come up with a really cool name for your train, what would you name it?

THINK ABOUT IT . . .

→ 31 ←

"Lots of people want to ride with you in the limousine, but what you want is someone who will take the bus with you when the limousine breaks down."

—*Oprah Winfrey, TV talk-show host*

What do these words mean for your life? *Talk about it with your parents or a teacher.*

— → 32 ← —

SUPPOSE THAT YOU had to go to school on Saturdays but in return you would be given off any one weekday of your choice . . . but it always had to be the same day. What day of the week would you want to have off?

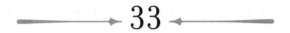

— → 33 ← —

EVERYONE KNOWS that before you can cut and eat a birthday cake, the birthday kid (or adult) has to blow out the candles. If you were asked to come up with a brand-new birthday tradition that would forever replace blowing out candles, what would you suggest as a new tradition?

34

IF YOU COULD change your last name to something completely different from what it is now, what would you choose as your new last name?

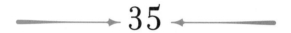

35

WHAT IS THE funniest thing you've ever seen someone's pet do?

36

IF a TOOTHPASTE company asked you to come up with an all-new flavor of toothpaste for kids, what flavor would you tell them to produce?

37

IF YOU COULD climb from the very bottom to the very top of anything in the world, what would you want to climb?

IMAGINATION IGNITER

→ 38 ←

If you were asked to design the ultimate miniature-golf hole, what would it look like?

39

IF YOU COULD have a challenging puzzle featuring the picture of any object or scene you wanted, what would people see when all the puzzle pieces were put together?

40

ALL RIGHT KIDS, be honest: What age does someone have to be for you to consider that person old?

41

IF YOU OWNED an ice-cream shop and had to put an edible surprise in the bottom of each ice-cream cone that you sold, what would you put in the bottom of each cone? (Example: a chocolate kiss.)

42

WHAT EVENT OR activity in the next few months are you looking forward to more than anything else?

43

IF YOU COULD convince a movie director to let your mom star in a movie, what type of role/character do you think she would play best? What type of role/character do you think your dad would play really well?

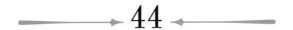

44

MORE THAN anything else, what one thing would you love to have in your bedroom that you currently do not have?

45

WHAT IS ONE event in American history that you would really like to learn a lot more about?

— 46 —

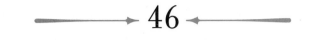

IF YOU WERE IN charge of building a
large carousel ride for a popular amusement
park, what type of animal(s) would visitors
to your carousel be riding? (You must
choose something other than horses.)

— 47 —

IN YOUR OPINION, what person that you
know has the funniest-sounding sneeze?

48

IF YOU WERE playing a game of hide-and-seek with your friends and your entire town was being used for the game, where in your town do you think would be the best hiding spot?

49

IF YOU COULD wake up tomorrow morning and be able to speak perfectly any language in the world, what language would you choose?

50

WHAT IS THE most exciting sports event you've ever attended?

51

WOULD YOU rather have school start earlier in the day and end earlier in the day, or start later in the day and end later in the day? (In other words, would you rather sleep later in the mornings or come home earlier in the afternoons?)

imagination igniter

Suppose that some people were building streets for an all-new town and they asked you to come up with names for the six main streets that will run through the community. The only catch is that all the names have to relate to one another in some way (for example, all names of states, all names of U.S. presidents, etc.). What would you name each of the six streets?

53

IF YOU HAD TO choose one or the other, would you rather be a diver who studies life in the ocean or a biologist who studies life in a tropical jungle?

54

IT'S ALWAYS FUN TO find buried treasure . . . but if you had to bury a treasure chest for someone else to dig up one day, with what things would you fill the treasure chest to make it a really cool "find" for the person who discovers it? (You may put into the chest anything at all except money.)

— 55 ←

WHAT ARE THREE things that, in your opinion, make your mom or dad the greatest parent in the whole world?

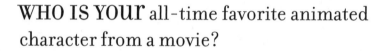

— 56 ←

WHO IS YOUR all-time favorite animated character from a movie?

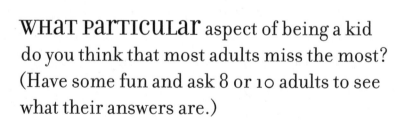

— 57 ←

WHAT PARTICULAR aspect of being a kid do you think that most adults miss the most? (Have some fun and ask 8 or 10 adults to see what their answers are.)

THINK ABOUT IT . . .

→ 58 ←

"100 percent of the shots you don't take don't go in."

—Wayne Gretzky, all-time leading scorer in the National Hockey League

What do these words mean for your life?
Talk about it with your parents or a teacher.

WHAT IS ONE thing you've accomplished that, back when you started trying to do it, you thought was going to be impossible to achieve? What lesson did you learn from this?

WHICH OF THE five senses (hearing, sight, smell, taste, and touch) do you think would be the hardest for you to live without? Which do you think would be the easiest for you to live without?

→ 61 ←

IF YOUR PARENTS told you that you had
their permission to start a club, what type of
club would it be, what would you name the
club, and what type of activities would you
and the other members do when meeting
together?

→ 62 ←

IF, DURING THE summer, you had to join
a circus, what particular act would you want
to do most of all?

63

TO THE BEST OF your memory, what is the most unusual food you've ever eaten? Did you like it? Why or why not? Would you try it again sometime?

64

IF YOU COULD permanently rid the world of any one type of insect or other creepy-crawly thing, which one would it be?

IMAGINATION IGNITER

→ 65 ←

If you were in charge of designing a really tall building for a U.S. city, what particular features would your building have that would make it stand out from other buildings?

—— 66 ——

WHAT IS THE strangest weather event you've ever witnessed in person? What type of weather event that you have not witnessed in person would you like to experience if you knew you would be perfectly safe?

—— 67 ——

IF YOU COULD have in your backyard a statue of anything or anyone at all, what or whom would the statue represent?

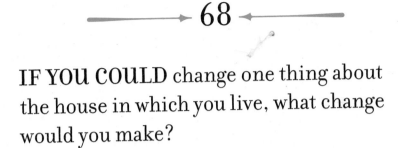

— **68** —

IF YOU COULD change one thing about the house in which you live, what change would you make?

— **69** —

IF YOU HAD TO BE a farmer, which of the following six animals would you want to raise most of all? Which would you want to raise least of all? (Choices: chickens, cows, goats, horses, pigs, sheep.)

imagination igniter

→ 70 ←

If your full name actually appeared in a dictionary, and the editors of that dictionary asked you to write a definition of who you are, what definition would you give for yourself?

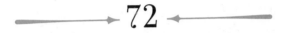

71

IF YOU COULD see any two animals in the world race against each other for one mile, which two animals would you choose?

72

WHICH OF THE following four "A's" would you want to be most of all? Which would you want to be least of all? (Choices: a famous actor, artist, athlete, or author.)

73

IF YOU COULD LearN more about any one state in our country (that is, learn more about its people, cities, geography, culture, etc.), which state would you choose?

THINK ABOUT IT . . .

→ 74 ←

"Speak when you are angry and you will make the best speech you will ever regret."

—*Ambrose Bierce, American writer*

What do these words mean for your life? *Talk about it with your parents or a teacher.*

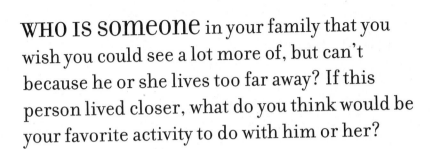

— 75 —

WHO IS someone in your family that you wish you could see a lot more of, but can't because he or she lives too far away? If this person lived closer, what do you think would be your favorite activity to do with him or her?

— 76 —

ADULTS usually greet one another by shaking hands or hugging. If you had to come up with a standard way for all kids around the country to greet one another (besides just saying "hi"), what would you suggest for a universal greeting?

77

IF YOU WERE AN airline pilot and could choose any two cities that your flight would connect, what two cities would you choose for your route?

78

OF ALL YOUR friends, which one do you think says or does the funniest things? What is the funniest thing this friend of yours has ever done? Which of the adults that you know says or does the funniest things? What is the funniest thing this adult has ever done?

IMAGINATION IGNITER

→ 79 ←

If you were in charge of planning from start to finish your family's next vacation, what type of trip would you plan? Be specific in as many of the details as you can (how you will get there, when you will go, where you will stay, what you will do each day, etc.).

→ 80 ←

WHICH IS YOUR favorite mode of transportation when taking a trip: airplane, car, or train? Of these three options, which is your least favorite way to travel on a trip? In your opinion, what are the advantages and disadvantages of each?

→ 81 ←

SUPPOSE THAT instead of having a big pile of leaves to jump into, you could have a big pile of anything else you wanted to jump into—anything at all! Taking a running start, what would you want to jump into most of all? (Example: a huge pile of fluffy whipped cream.)

82

IF YOU HAD TO rearrange the letters of your first name to give yourself a new name, what would it be and how would you pronounce the new name?

83

WHO IS THE TALLEST person you've ever met? Do you think it would be fun to be that tall? Why or why not?

84

IF SOMETHING OTHER than the standard cuckoo could pop out of a clock to announce the time each hour, what would you want it to be and what sound would it make?

— 85 —

IF YOU COULD create a special sandwich of your choice, putting anything you wanted between two slices of bread, what would you put on the sandwich?

— 86 —

WHEN YOU'RE having fun with your friends or your family, who is your favorite person or character that you like to pretend to be?

WHAT PERSON above all others in American history do you think had the greatest impact on our country? Why?

WHAT IS something that many adults seem to really enjoy doing that to you, as a kid, looks extremely boring?

IMAGINATION IGNITER

→ 89 ←

If a beverage company asked you to come up with a new type of soda, what flavor would it be and what would you call it?

WHAT IS YOUR favorite number, 0 through 9? Why? What is your least favorite number, 0 through 9? Why?

——→ 91 ←——

SUPPOSE THAT BY snapping your fingers you could instantly become twice as smart as you are in any subject of your choice . . . but at the same time you would have to become half as smart as you currently are in another subject. Would you be willing to sacrifice some knowledge in one subject in order to instantly gain knowledge in another subject? Why or why not?

IF YOU COULD change or add any law in your town or city, what would it be?

IF YOU COULD SET the time for when you have to go to bed each night, what time would you make it? Is there anything you really like that you would be willing to give up completely in order to get a later bedtime each night?

—— 94 ——

WHAT IS THE most exciting/fun car trip that you've ever taken?

—— 95 ——

IF YOU COULD attach a swing to anything in the world and could be guaranteed that you would be perfectly safe while swinging on it, where would you put your swing?

THINK ABOUT IT . . .

→ 96 ←

"Thinking is the hardest work there is, which is probably the reason why so few people do it."

—*Henry Ford, American automobile manufacturer*

What do these words mean for your life? *Talk about it with your parents or a teacher.*

SUPPOSE THAT someone gave you the following balls—not to be used as part of an organized sport, but just to have fun with around the house or in the yard. For that purpose, how would you rank these eight balls in order from your favorite to your least favorite? (Choices: baseball, basketball, bowling ball, football, golf ball, ping-pong ball, soccer ball, tennis ball.)

IF YOU COULD invite any famous person in the world to come to your house for an evening and have dinner with you, whom would you invite and what type of food would you have?

ALTHOUGH WE sometimes look at famous people and wish that we could be like they are, what do you think would be some of the big drawbacks (disadvantages) of being famous?

WHAT IS YOUR favorite time of the day? What is your favorite day of the week? What is your favorite day of the year? What is your favorite week of the year? What is your favorite month of the year? What is your favorite season of the year?

imagination igniter

If you were the captain of a new passenger ship and had to come up with a creative name for your ocean-going vessel, what would you name it?

IF ONE OF YOUR friends challenged you and some other kids to see who could eat the most scoops of ice cream at one time, how many scoops of your favorite ice cream do you think you could eat? Do you think you'd feel sick after eating that much? In reality, what is the most ice cream you've ever eaten at one time?

IF YOU HAD TO come up with an animal besides the bunny to serve as the Easter mascot, what animal would you choose to leave baskets and eggs on Easter morning? (Example: the Easter seal.)

104

IF YOU COULD change one thing about the weather or the seasons—any one thing at all—what change would you make?

105

IF YOU COULD float slowly and softly in a hot-air balloon over any famous place in the world, what would you choose to look down on from the air?

106

If you were asked to help design a new car for a famous automobile company, what unique and fun features would you suggest that they add to the new car?

→ 107 ←

IF YOU HAD TO spend four weeks this summer at a camp for kids, where in the country would you want the camp located, and what would you want to be the theme/focus of the camp?

→ 108 ←

WHAT IS YOUR favorite color when it comes to food?

→ 109 ←

IF YOU WERE PUT IN charge of planning your school's next field trip/outing, where would your class go?

110

WHICH DO YOU think would be more fun to live in for one week: a tree house or a cave?

111

WHAT IS YOUR favorite thing to do to help your mom or dad get ready for company coming to visit?

112

IF YOU COULD DO something (by yourself or with your friends) to try and cheer up all the sick children at a hospital, what would you do for them?

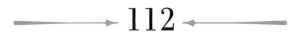

THINK ABOUT IT . . .

→ 113 ←

"To be blind is bad, but worse it is to have eyes and not to see."
—*Helen Keller, blind and deaf American writer and speaker*

What do these words mean for your life?
Talk about it with your parents or a teacher.

→ 114 ←

IF YOU COULD put anything at all into pancake batter to make a special type of pancake, what would you put in it?

→ 115 ←

FOR YOUR NEXT birthday, would you rather receive just one large gift (in terms of size) or five small gifts (in terms of size)?

→ 116 ←

WHAT IS YOUR all-time favorite animal (real, not animated) from a movie?

IF YOU COULD create a great Web site that gave people a huge amount of information on any particular topic of your choice, what topic/subject would your Web site feature?

IMAGINATION IGNITER

→ 118 ←

If you were asked to create an all-new, never-before-seen toy that would be sold in toy stores around the country, what would this new toy be called and what would it do?

— 119 →

IF IT WEREN'T FOR their terrible smell, skunks might actually be popular little animals (they really are quite cute). If you could make skunks smell like anything at all that the average person wouldn't mind, what would you make a skunk smell like?

— 120 →

IF YOU COULD celebrate your half birthday by doing anything at all that would fit the season in which your half birthday falls, what would you want to do most of all? (Example: if your half birthday falls in January, you could have a sledding party with your friends.)

— 121 —

WHAT IS THE most fun event you've ever been a part of or attended? (The event can be something at school, something with your family, with your friends . . . anything at all.)

— 122 —

FROM WHAT YOU know of it, what country's way of life do you think would be the hardest for you to get used to if you had to move to that country? Do you think it would be just as hard for people from that country to live in the United States?

imagination igniter

Suppose that for your next birthday all the gifts that you receive have to begin with the same letter. Which letter would you choose and what are three gifts you would like that start with this letter?

— → 124 ← —

YUM-YUM! WHAT is your favorite type of candy? What is your favorite type of cookie? What is your favorite type of cake? What is your favorite type of pie? What is your favorite type of ice cream?

— → 125 ← —

OUT OF ALL THE things you have and are able to do in your life, what are you thankful for most of all?

126

WHAT IS THE most fun you've ever had at someone else's birthday party?

127

WHAT IS YOUR favorite summertime food (that is, a food that you generally eat only during the summer months)?

IMAGINATION IGNITER

→ 128 ←

If someone from Canada brought you a moose for a pet, what would you name it?

129

ALL OF US LIKE TO play games that we win a lot, but what is your favorite game to play that you don't necessarily win a lot? In your opinion, how important is it to like to do things in life even if you're not really good at them?

130

WHAT IS ONE food that your mom or dad thinks is one of the best things in the world that you, on the other hand, absolutely can't stand to eat? Do you think you might change your mind about this food as you get older?

— 131 —

IF YOU COULD receive for your next birthday any one intangible gift (that is, a gift you can't physically touch with your hands), what would you want most of all? (Example: permission to watch all the TV you want for a week.)

— 132 —

IF IT COULD somehow happen, do you think it would be really fun to have a huge snowstorm right in the middle of July (a snowstorm that would bring at least a foot of snow and cold weather for, say, one week)? Why or why not?

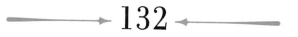

THINK ABOUT IT . . .

→ **133** ←

"Our greatest weakness lies in giving up.
The most certain way to succeed is
always to try one more time."

—*Thomas Edison, American inventor*

What do these words mean for your life?
Talk about it with your parents or a teacher.

→ 134 ←

IF YOU HAD TO LIST the following activities from one to six, with one being your favorite thing to do and six being your least favorite thing to do, how would you rank them? Assume that in all the cases you could have a friend join you. (Choices: going to your favorite restaurant for dinner, going to your favorite store at the mall, going to a zoo, going to watch your favorite sports team play, going to see a movie at the theater, and going to a swimming pool.)

→ 135 ←

IF YOU HAD TO "dress-up" a jack-o'-lantern, how would you decorate it and what would you put on it to make it different from any other carved pumpkin?

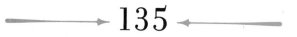

— 136 —

YOU'VE PROBABLY seen or heard of state fairs and other summer events where they have contests to see who can eat the most of something (like watermelon or pie). If you had to choose the type of food that would be eaten in a contest, what type would you choose? (You can pick any type of food that you want, but assume that you also will have to participate in the event!)

— 137 —

IF YOU HAD TO SIT down and interview some of your family members about what their childhood was like, who would you be most interested in interviewing? What would you be most curious to learn about their life as a child?

IMAGINATION IGNITER

→ 138 ←

If a big city close to you was building a brand-new aquarium that people could visit and they asked you to come up with one of the exhibits for this new aquarium, what type of exhibit would you design and what would be some of its most unusual or interesting features?

139

WHAT IS ONE activity you did for the first time ever this year that you really hope you get the chance to do again sometime soon?

140

IF YOU WERE A teacher, what are three rules that you would insist that your students obey?

141

IF YOU WERE playing a game with your friends in which the goal was to try and hide a cooking pot somewhere inside your house, what do you think would be the best hiding spot for the pot?

142

IF YOU COULD add anything at all to the typical playground that would make it far more exciting or interesting, what would you add?

143

IF YOU HAD TO describe your personality in terms of a forest animal, what animal would best describe it?

144

WHAT IS YOUR favorite food to smell while it's baking in the oven?

SUPPOSE THAT you had to sit at a small table for one full hour, and on that table you could choose to have either three paper clips or three pennies—absolutely nothing else. Which would you rather have to help you pass the time while you are seated at the table?

146

SUPPOSE THAT FOR the next school year, your school would start its classes one full month earlier than it normally does . . . but to balance it off, it would end the school year one full month earlier than it normally does. How would you like this arrangement?

147

SUPPOSE THAT FOR the next school year, your school would start its classes one full month later than it normally does . . . but to balance it off, it would have classes go one full month longer at the end of the school year. How would you feel about an arrangement like this?

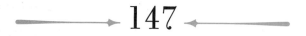

IMAGINATION IGNITER

→ 148 ←

If you were in charge of organizing a special Fourth of July celebration for your town, what specific events would you plan to make it a really fun and memorable day for everyone?

149

WHAT IS THE best gift your mom ever got in her life? What is the best gift your dad ever got in his life? (If you aren't sure, here's your chance to ask them.)

150

ALL THE students at school have been asked to wear an ornament around their neck for five days, an ornament that best represents or symbolizes who each student is. What would your ornament look like?

IMAGINATION IGNITER

151

If you could change the ending to any book you've read, what book's ending would you change and what would the new ending be?

152

IF YOU COULD GO to a manufacturing/ assembly plant and see, from start to finish, exactly how any one thing is made or put together, what would you want to see?

153

IF YOUR PARENTS gave you permission to take any piece of furniture in the house and move it permanently into your own bedroom, what piece of furniture would you choose?

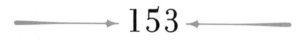

→ 154 ←

IN YOUR OPINION, what is the most exciting thing that you've learned in school so far this year?

→ 155 ←

IF YOU WERE given a piece of land about the size of a school gymnasium and had to plant a garden on that land, what would you want to plant and grow in this garden of yours?

THINK ABOUT IT . . .

→ 156 ←

"More people are ruined by victory,
I imagine, than by defeat."
—*Eleanor Roosevelt, U.S. delegate to the United Nations*

What do these words mean for your life?
Talk about it with your parents or a teacher.

— 157 —

ROUGHLY HOW long before your actual birthday do you start to think about your special day? How long before your birthday do you really, really get excited about it?

— 158 —

WHAT IS THE most fun you've ever had doing something outside in the rain? Did your parents think it was fun, too?

— 159 —

HAVE YOU EVER wanted a toy really badly and then, after getting it and playing with it a few times, hardly ever again played with that toy? If so, what toy was it and why do you think you got tired of it so quickly?

WHAT IS something you always used to love to do that, during the last year or so, you feel like you've outgrown or lost all interest in doing?

IF YOU COULD have in your yard a tall tree with leaves of any color you wanted, what color leaves would this unusual tree have?

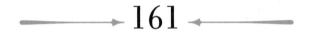

162

IF THE "SPIRIT" OF any one holiday could last all year long, what holiday would you want it to be? (When we say spirit, we mean how that holiday makes people feel inside and how it makes them act toward other people.)

163

SUPPOSE THAT your school was having "Noise Day," a day for which every student was told to bring something to school that made noise. The only rule is that it has to be something that you can carry in your own hands (sorry, no airplanes from the airport!). What would you want to bring to school for everyone to hear?

imagination igniter

Many nightly news programs for adults have segments, such as international news, politics, money, health, sports, weather, etc. If you were in charge of creating a nightly nationwide newscast specifically aimed at kids your age, what would be the various segments of your news? Whom would you choose to serve as the anchor (that is, the main reporter) of the newscast?

— 165 —

IF YOU COULD TAKE any man-made object located in another city and move that object to your own city or town, what would you want to see moved to the area where you live? (Example: if you live in a small town somewhere, you could move the Statue of Liberty to your town.)

— 166 —

WHICH OF THE following activities do you think is the most fun to do: coloring Easter eggs, carving a Halloween pumpkin, or decorating a Christmas tree? (Remember: This question isn't asking you what your favorite holiday is; it's asking you what your favorite activity is.)

167

IF YOUR PARENTS allowed you to decorate the front door to your house, how would you decorate it?

168

IF A BUBBLE BATH company offered to give you a full year's supply of bubble bath in any scent that you wanted, what would you want the bubble bath to smell like?

169

IF YOU WERE president of the United States, what do you think would be the most difficult part of your job? What do you think would be the best part of having that job?

IMAGINATION IGNITER

→ 170 ←

If you were asked to redesign the American flag, what would the new flag look like?

OF ALL THE thousands of words you probably know at this point in your life, what do you think is the coolest-sounding word of all?

WHAT IS ONE BOOK OR story you've read that you would like to see made into an animated movie? (Of course, make sure you pick a book that has not already been made into a movie.)

IF YOU WERE ON A train ride, which of these two would be more exciting for you: Going over a long, high bridge or going through a long, dark tunnel?

— 174 —

IN YOUR OPINION, what are three ways that parents can best show their kids how much they love them? On the other hand, what are three ways that kids can best show their parents how much they love them?

— 175 —

IF YOU COULD TRULY live through any one scene from a movie you have watched, what movie scene would you want to experience in real life?

— 176 —

IF YOU COULD PLANT in your backyard a tree that could grow on its branches anything at all that you wanted—anything except money—what would you want your tree to grow?

→ 177 ←

IF someone gave you $250 as a gift tomorrow, which of the following would best describe what you would do with the money: spend it all right away on things you want, spend a little bit at a time but spend it all within a couple of months, or save it all for something in the more distant future?

→ 178 ←

IF your had your parent's permission to put in a blender any three types of food you wanted—just to see what it would look like and taste like—what three foods would you blend together?

THINK ABOUT IT . . .

→ 179 ←

"A life is not important except in the impact it has on other lives."

—*Jackie Robinson, first African American to play baseball in the Major Leagues*

What do these words mean for your life? *Talk about it with your parents or a teacher.*

180

WOULD YOU rather live in a house next to the ocean or live in a house up in the mountains? Why?

181

IF YOU COULD bring to life any imaginary animal from any story you've ever read, what animal would you like to see alive?

IF YOU HaD TO move the capital of the
United States from Washington, D.C., to
another city in America, what city would
you choose? Why do you think your choice
would be a good spot to have the capital?

IF YOU COULD PUT anything really
unusual in your backyard for you and your
friends to play in and around, what would you
put there? (Example: an empty railroad car.)

imagination igniter

Some local firefighters are holding a contest to see who can come up with the best name for a new Dalmatian at the fire station. What would you suggest as a name for this friendly firehouse dog?

IF YOU COULD have 1,000 of anything red, what would you want most of all? What if you could have 1,000 of anything white? (Example: 1,000 strawberries and 1,000 snowballs.)

WHAT DO YOU think is the most important thing that friends can do for one another? Why do you think that this is so important?

→ 187 ←

REGARDING something that your parents gave you permission to do, what do you personally think is the most dangerous thing you've ever done? (Example: skiing down a steep mountain slope.)

→ 188 ←

IN YOUR OPINION, what is the most interesting guided tour you've ever been on?

→ 189 ←

IF, INSTEAD OF actually writing out your name, you now had to "sign" your name with a drawing of something, what would you draw each time to represent your name?

→ 190 ←

IF YOU COULD TAKE any animal at all and have it make the sound of a completely different animal, what two animals would you bring together? (Example: a turtle that oinks and grunts like a pig.)

→ 191 ←

WHAT IS THE MOST unusual thing you've ever discovered in your yard (or anywhere else for that matter)?

→ 192 ←

WHAT IS YOUR favorite thing to do on rainy days in the summer?

→ 193 ←

IF YOU COULD build a bridge to connect any two points you wanted, what would your bridge connect and how might you design the bridge to make it unusual?

→ 194 ←

IF YOU COULD BE any age at all for one week, what age would you choose? Why? Assume that you would have to experience all the responsibilities that go along with being that age.

IMAGINATION IGNITER

→ 195 ←

If you had to create a brand-new word that would be added to the dictionary, how would this new word be spelled, how would it be pronounced, and what would be its definition?

196

WHAT IS THE MOST awesome machine that you've ever seen? Specifically, what about this machine makes it so incredible, in your opinion?

197

WHAT WOULD YOU think about having a birthday only once every four years? Three years out of four, February has only 28 days. Every fourth year, February is given one extra day on the calendar—February 29—we call this a leap year. So, if you were born on February 29, you'd technically only have a birthday once every four years! If you were one of these people, how or when would you celebrate your birthday the other three years?

198

YOUR PRIZE FOR winning a contest is to get a bucket filled to the top with one of the following things: a bucket of soft sand, a bucket of shiny marbles, or a bucket of fresh oranges. Which would you choose as your prize?

199

WHICH OF THESE DO you think would be scarier: to be swimming in the ocean and suddenly see a shark, or to be walking in the woods and suddenly hear a bear growl?

200

WHAT IS YOUR favorite thing to do or favorite game to play when standing in a circle with other kids?

THINK ABOUT IT . . .

→ 201 ←

"Wherever we look on this earth, the opportunities always take shape within the problems."

—*Nelson Rockefeller, Vice President of the United States*

What do these words mean for your life? *Talk about it with your parents or a teacher.*

— → 202 ← —

IN YOUR OPINION, what would be the most enjoyable thing about being a dog? What would be the most difficult or annoying thing about being a dog?

— → 203 ← —

IF YOU WERE GIVEN an unlimited quantity and variety of LEGO blocks in order to build a model of anything you wanted—anything at all—what would you build with all these colored blocks?

— → 204 ← —

IN YOUR OPINION, what is the silliest-looking piece of fruit?

→ 205 ←

IF YOU COULD receive a personal letter written to you from anyone in the world, whose letter would you like to find in your mailbox one day?

→ 206 ←

IF YOU COULD wake up every morning and discover that something took care of itself overnight—something that you normally have to do yourself—what one thing above all else would you want to find done each morning when you roll out of bed? (Example: your teeth would be brushed.)

imagination igniter

If a local radio station offered to let you have your own 30-minute show in the morning, five days a week, what type of show would you have? Be as specific as you can.

208

IF rain could fall in any color, what color would you choose? (Imagine, after the rain, huge puddles of water in this color, too.)

209

where is your favorite place of all to go and play?

210

IF YOU were IN charge of designing a new postage stamp, what or whom would you put on this new stamp?

IMAGINATION IGNITER

Many books have a table of contents at the beginning (that is, a page that lists the titles of all the chapters to come in the book). If someone were writing a book all about you and your life so far and you knew that the book needed to have six chapters, what would you suggest as the title for each of the six chapters?

DO YOU KNOW why your parents chose the name for you that they did? If you're not sure, take this opportunity to find out. Ask them if there were any other names that they were thinking about as well.

ALL rIGHT, KIDS, get those creative caps on. Now it's your turn to come up with some fun and thought-provoking questions. Use the following pages to write down any questions you'd like . . . and remember to share those questions with your friends and family!

MY QUESTIONS:

Got a question of your own that you'd like to send us? How about giving us your answer to one or more of the questions in this book? We'd love to hear from you. Write us a letter, put it in the mail, and we'll be sure to get it . . . as long as you address it as follows:

Bret and Paul, The Question Guys™
P.O. BOX 340, YANKTON, SD 57078

ABOUT THE AUTHORS

Bret Nicholaus and Paul Lowrie, The Question Guys™, are the authors of the national bestselling question books *The Conversation Piece* and *The Christmas Conversation Piece*. Altogether, they have written over 3,000 questions that have appeared in ten books. This is their second question book written specifically for young readers. Bret Nicholaus and his family live in the Chicago area. Paul Lowrie resides in South Dakota.